The Case for a Basic Income
by Robert Jameson

Warning/Disclaimer:

Please bear in mind that this is a book intended to explore ideas. It contains intelligently-considered opinions, but should not be relied upon as a source of factual information of any kind.

Contents

The Basics

In its simplest form, a Basic Income is a regular, tax-free, fixed amount of money paid to every citizen of a country. It would probably be paid once a week and should be sufficient to meet people's essential needs.

Its defining characteristic is that, unlike almost every other form of benefit payment, it is entirely non-means-tested. It doesn't matter what your income is. You don't have to prove you need the money. You don't have to prove you're looking for work. Every citizen gets it - regardless of their circumstances.

It is a simple idea, but it is also a radical idea, because it would involve a dramatic departure from the way state benefits are currently distributed in most countries.

Perhaps what makes it a particularly interesting and fascinating idea, however, is the fact that it appears to provoke such a vast range of different - and sometimes rather extreme - reactions.

To some people, it is a wonderful idea - not just a policy with many great practical benefits, but an idea with the potential to transform the very nature of our economies - and societies - for the better.

To others, it is a terrible idea, worthy only of derision and ridicule. And some even regard it as a dangerous idea - even as one that could precipitate economic disaster and societal collapse.

A basic income could represent a revolution - for good or evil - according to who you speak to. So, is it the key to a brighter future - or is it ridiculous, unaffordable and dangerous, as some people claim?

Well, I'm not going to make the answer a subject of cheap suspense. I'm clear that I think Basic Income is an excellent idea, capable of helping us deal effectively with all sorts of problems and greatly enhancing our potential for economic success.

Unfortunately, debates about the basic income are often quickly closed down by criticisms that rely on false or misleading assertions. People are frightened off the idea by claims and arguments which are seriously flawed and based on misunderstandings. We shouldn't allow ourselves to be held back in this way.

The case for a basic income is often poorly understood and sometimes poorly presented. Although the most prominent arguments against it are deeply flawed, even some of its main supporters seem unsure on key questions - such as how it could be paid for.

In this book, I will explore what the key benefits of a basic income system might be. I will also be dissecting the main arguments made against the idea of a basic income and I will be debunking some of the common myths that are used to ridicule the idea. And I will consider how a basic income might best be introduced.

Of course, there may be perfectly reasonable people who oppose the basic income - but our debates should be intelligent, informed debates. We should be debating the real benefits and potential drawbacks of a basic income - not relying on ludicrous myths that have little or no basis in economic reality. I want to offer my expertise as a skilled economist to help people on all sides of the debate to separate reasonable concerns from scaremongering nonsense.

Different people may mean slightly different things when they refer to the idea of a basic income. The basic idea is that it will be paid to all working-age adults. But will it also be paid to pensioners? Will it be paid to children?

So, to avoid confusion and help us focus on the fundamentals, rather than the details of different potential schemes, I want to be clear that, in this book, I'm going to be referring to a very simple basic income system that would work as follows:

Every working-age adult citizen would receive the same basic income payment every week. A smaller basic income, known simply as Child Benefit, will be paid for each child. Pensioners will receive a higher basic income, known as the Basic Pension.

There are slightly different, alternative arrangements that could be made and which could still be referred to as a basic income system, but this is the system I will be referring to in this book.

The idea of a basic income - also known as a 'Citizen's Income' is not a new one. And when it is occasionally proposed, it is often hastily dismissed and largely forgotten about, sometimes for many years. And yet it is an idea that, no matter how savagely it is criticised or ridiculed, nevertheless keeps on cropping back up again.

It is currently experiencing one of these resurgent phases, with the idea under serious consideration in a number of countries, with some countries planning trial schemes and a number of political parties expressing their support for the idea - at least in principle.

And the reason the idea keeps cropping back up again and again is that it is an idea that is fundamentally appealing, for a wide range of different reasons, to many people of different political persuasions.

Some people - many of whom might be on the traditional left of the political spectrum - see it as a great weapon against poverty - a guarantee that every citizen of a country will have enough to live on, without the humiliation of means-testing.

At the same time, the idea is supported by some people on the traditional right of the political spectrum - people who, for example, might see it as a means to shrink state bureaucracy and reduce government interference in our lives.

The idea also receives criticism from both left and right - and I'm not going to pretend that introducing a basic income would be without difficulties or controversies. The potential benefits of a basic income system, however, are very important and valuable ones - as this book will seek to demonstrate - so I think everyone should at least understand what those potential benefits might be and what the general case for a basic income is, so that we can have a proper, intelligent debate about this hugely important opportunity.

The Benefits

The potential benefits of establishing a basic income system are, in fact, numerous and wide-ranging. Yet, I suspect that, at the time of writing, most people are either completely unaware of the idea or, if they have heard of it, have given little thought to what the full potential benefits are or how transformative for our society they might prove to be.

Yes, some people have considered the idea of a basic income, but will still argue against it. They may claim it would be too costly, too ambitious or even dangerous. Such concerns should be rigorously considered - but anyone who refuses to consider and appreciate the possible benefits of a basic income, is foolish in the extreme. Potentially, the benefits are enormous.

This chapter is simply going to outline some of the most straightforward practical benefits of a basic income system - and I'll deal with some of the other benefits in later chapters.

Obviously, the central purpose of a basic income is a very important and stark one; to stop people starving to death in the streets. Clearly, many developed nations already have a benefits system that (on the whole) manages to achieve this aim - but a basic income has many advantages over our current means-tested benefits.

For many people, the great advantages of a basic income lie not in some sort of ideological vision, but rather in the fact that a basic income could bring about a monumental simplification of our tax and benefit system - a simplification that could enable huge improvements in efficiency and huge cost savings.

These cost savings would arise from the fact that basic income is an incredibly simple system to administrate, yet would be able to replace a huge swathe of complicated benefit systems currently in operation - and free us all from paying for the huge administration costs that go with them.

With a basic income system in place, there would no longer be any need for unemployment benefit. There would no longer be any need for sickness benefits paid to people who are unable to work. There would be no need for tax credits or 'universal credit' or income support. Incapacity benefit, carers' allowances, some (but not all) disability benefits, maternity allowances, child benefit, council tax benefit - no longer needed!

The unemployed, the sick, the disabled, the heavily pregnant, carers - would all be receiving the basic income, just like everyone else. Other than in exceptional cases, they would already have the means to pay for essentials and would not need additional benefits.

Many of our existing benefits are complicated and costly to administer, because they rely very heavily on means-testing. Many thousands of civil servants have to be employed to follow complicated rules to assess who is or isn't entitled to these benefits - and, if people are entitled to benefits, just how much money they are entitled to receive.

And different benefits use different means-testing regimes, with different rules and different assessment procedures. Here in the UK, for example, someone whose income is assessed for tax credit purposes may also have their incomes assessed, using different rules, through an entirely separate system with its own separate and complicated set of assessment procedures and managed by a separate set of administrators, for council tax benefit purposes. They might have yet more, separate sets of means-testing imposed for other benefits, such as disability benefits.

It's incredibly wasteful to subject one person to several, parallel sets of means-testing. Indeed, the obvious option of having a basic income system, means that any such means-testing is wasteful and unnecessary. Expensive regulatory systems, operating in parallel, duplicating essentially the same function - it's madness! And, of course, these wasteful means-testing procedures often have to be repeated for each official assessment period or whenever a claimant has a 'change in circumstances.'

The means-testing industry of bureaucracy is vast, expensive and intrusive. Applications, supporting documents, hundreds of millions of letters, e-mails and phone calls every year, armies of administrators, claimant interviews, reams of regulations, complicated sets of assessment procedures, appeals procedures, changes of circumstances, fraud investigations, reviews - and vast, complicated computer systems, developed and installed at great expense and maintained by an army of technicians!

And the administrators have managers to oversee their work. The managers have managers - and their managers have managers. And they all have training days and Powerpoint presentations and committee meetings and appraisals and performance reviews. They get paid and promoted and redeployed from one post to another.

All in all, it's an ongoing orgy of administrative excess - that we taxpayers have to pay for. Billions

11

and billions of pounds of administrative expenses incurred every year - that would no longer be necessary with a basic income.

But the civil service salaries are just the tip of the iceberg when it comes to assessing the full economic cost of means-testing. Much of the bureaucratic burden of all these different benefits is not directly borne by the government or paid for through taxes.

Very probably, most of the man hours wasted by our complicated benefits system, are provided by people who aren't employed by the government. When an unemployed person has to travel to a job centre in order to 'sign on' and claim their unemployment benefit, this might only take 5 minutes of an official's time. The unemployed person, however, might have to travel for half an hour or more to get to the unemployment office, might have to wait to be seen when they get there and then spend another half an hour or so travelling home.

For every hour that a bureaucrat spends checking a claim form, there may be several hours spent by the claimants completing the claim form and gathering all the necessary documentational evidence to support their claim. So, the cost savings, in terms of man hours, may be far larger than many people might imagine.

In assessing how valuable an opportunity basic income represents, it is important to appreciate the following: We all ought to be aware that our lives are dogged by excessive complexity - that the public sector is plagued by seemingly endless sets of massively complicated regulations. We all ought to know that we are in desperate need of simplification. Even the government occasionally seems to recognise this - and talks about the desperate need to cut red tape.

Yet, whilst new government policies are often presented as simplifications, they very rarely turn out that way. They may start out as a slight or even moderate simplification of existing systems, but through the whole process of consultation, review and implementation, all sorts of modifications and additions are made to the original proposals - often for political purposes - and, by the time the new system is in place, it is often actually much more complicated than the system it replaced. Worse, new systems often end up working in parallel to old ones and don't replace them at all.

But, in terms of simplification, the basic income is not tinkering around at the edges, but dramatic, game-changing simplification. It offers a real prospect of a genuine revolution in simplification, in efficiency and in the reduction of costly bureaucracy.

And not only would basic income provide a dramatic simplification of our benefits system at the point of introduction, it will also provide a defence against future complications and future uncertainty.

Once basic income is established, it very significantly reduces the risk of further upheavals to our benefits system. This is because a basic income system is, in many ways, the ultimate benefits system. You can't really get any simpler. You can't really get any more efficient.

Yes, there will be changes in the level of basic income - but the fundamentals of the basic income system can remain unchanged. It is the sort of thing that, no matter how much some people might resist its introduction, once it's introduced, it would most likely be here to stay. It would probably seem completely nonsensical to choose to return to costly means-testing once it had already been proven that means-testing is not necessary.

Once the scare stories have proved to be nonsense, the basic income would be here to stay. This would bring stability. It would improve people's lives by reducing uncertainty and enable people to plan more effectively for the future.

And, very importantly, it wouldn't be just our benefits system that would be simplified by the introduction of a basic income. A basic income would also present a huge opportunity to dramatically simplify our tax system too. All sorts of complications in the tax system, including various tax reliefs, deemed necessary given our current benefits system, would be made redundant by the introduction of a basic income system.

And basic income would also enable a dramatic simplification of our pension system. A Basic Pension would replace other state pension schemes - and could despatch to history the huge administrative hassles and costs that go with them. (More on these subjects in later chapters!).

It probably wouldn't be overstating the case to say that a basic income could have a substantial impact on the efficiency with which we run our entire society.

I wouldn't argue that, with a basic income system, everyone currently receiving benefits would be financially better off than they are now. Many people will be. Others might have less than they do now.

But even many of those who do receive less actual money, will still be better off in many important and substantial ways. They won't have to sign on. They won't have to apply for benefits. They won't have to undergo means-testing or interviews. Most disability assessments will no longer be needed.

And when people who rely on benefits seek jobs or seek to increase their hours or gain better-paid work, a basic income system will better support them to do so, as they won't lose their basic income payments as their earnings increase.

A basic income system would be a kinder, more understanding, less judgemental benefits system that simply recognises that, whoever you are, whatever your background, whatever your circumstances, you need to eat and you need a bed to sleep on.

A basic income system would be better for people in poverty and better for the people who foot the bill - because it is so simple, efficient and cost-effective.

Is It Affordable?

One of the biggest barriers to implementing a basic income system is that it is an idea that, for various reasons, attracts a lot of scare stories. Chief amongst these is the claim that it is a ludicrously unaffordable idea. By the end of this chapter, I hope it will be clear why the arguments behind these claims of unaffordability are fundamentally flawed.

As an economist, I can tell you, with a very high degree of confidence, that it is not unaffordable at all. In fact, the belief that it is unaffordable is usually based on a serious lack of understanding of some fairly basic economics.

It is true, of course, that, at first glance, the basic income does indeed look like it would be very expensive - because it obviously involves paying every citizen thousands of pounds per year.

In stark terms, paying a basic income of £80 a week to every resident adult citizen of the UK, and a smaller amount to children, could rack up an annual bill of over £200 billion.

It does sound astronomical. Surely unaffordable? But this is where you might be in need of an economist to explain the various reasons why it is nothing like as big a problem as you would instinctively think it was.

For one thing, most of that money is already being spent under our current benefits system. It is already being paid out each year in state pensions, in unemployment benefit, in tax credits, in disability payments, in child benefit and in many other forms of benefit. Fundamentally, the basic income is a replacement for a whole range of other benefits - not something that has to be paid for in addition to those benefits.

Plus, there are sizeable savings to be taken into account - savings that result from the extensive bureaucracy that will no longer be needed. So it isn't an extra £200 billion that must be funded through extra taxation - it is only a fraction of that amount.

There will, in all likelihood, be a remaining sum to be generated through taxation. However, that doesn't mean we have to resort to massively hiking tax rates or introducing inventive new forms of taxation.

In fact, some of the most important tax changes will follow on quite naturally from the idea of establishing a basic income and could raise very significant sums without any great upheaval, given that they would be introduced alongside the basic income.

The most obvious of these tax changes is merely the fact that personal tax allowances will no longer be needed.

The UK, like many other countries, allows each worker a personal tax allowance - an amount they can earn before paying any income tax. This system is there to recognise that you need a certain amount to live on - and can't really afford to pay income tax until your income reaches a certain level. So, the government refrains from charging you income tax until after you've earned the basic amount you need to live on.

But, with a basic income, this all changes. The basic income is a clear and obvious replacement for a system of personal tax allowances. So, these allowances will no longer be needed.

Personal tax allowances can simply be scrapped

altogether, so that people can pay income tax, at a reasonable rate, on every pound they earn. That would seem perfectly fair and reasonable, given that every citizen will already have a living allowance in the form of the basic income.

Additionally, if the basic rate of income tax were to be raised by a moderate amount, that again would seem far more reasonable than it would have done without a basic income. If everyone already receives a basic income sufficient to meet their essential needs, then a 25% or even 30% starting rate of income tax seems fairly reasonable. Even at 30%, with no personal allowances, every citizen gets a basic, trouble-free, worry-free, hassle-free, non-means-tested income and gets to keep a substantial majority of any additional money they earn.

On the whole, replacing tax allowances would be a very positive move, because tax allowances are a seriously flawed system. Whilst they protect the essential income of workers, they don't help people who can't find work or who are unable to work or who are refused work because of other people's prejudices. They don't help people who are too ill to work or too old to work or too busy raising children to be able to work in a conventional job.

Because of these weaknesses, it becomes necessary to have a range of other benefits to account for such circumstances. And those other benefits can be expensive to administrate. This is why a basic income is often considered a far superior system for preventing people being unable to feed themselves or pay for other essentials.

Another tax change that might naturally accompany a basic income would be with regard to pension tax relief. In order to encourage people to invest in pension schemes and to assist them in building up a pension pot, the government in the UK (as in other countries) operates a system of pension tax relief. In particular, a person may qualify for a reduction in their income tax bill or an income tax rebate, if some of their income is paid into a pension scheme.

Since the basic pension part of a basic income scheme would ensure every citizen has a pension to live on in retirement, there would be far less need for the government to use tax breaks to encourage additional pension provision. Pension tax relief represents a substantial cost - in the form of lost revenue - to the treasury. With a basic income system, it would no longer be needed.

The government might still want to use some tax breaks to encourage saving - in order to steer the economy towards important investment activities, but these could be in the form of more generalised savings schemes, perhaps over much shorter periods than a pension scheme.

Because people won't then have to wait so long to get their hands on their own money, the incentive for them to save may be much stronger and more effective than our current pension schemes, even though the size of the tax break might be significantly less.

Pensions schemes often involve saving for so far in the future that, given all the uncertainty about changes in pension rules and life circumstances that can occur in that time, people can have little confidence about what their pension will really be worth or when they will be able to get access to it. There is so much risk involved, that many people see little point in investing in such schemes. Shorter-term schemes, therefore, could be much more effective ways of encouraging people to save more.

So, it seems likely that many of the people who say a basic income is unaffordable, are simply not taking into account the full range of changes that would accompany the introduction of a basic income. Although, to be fair, some of the people who have championed a basic income, have also failed to highlight or understand the range of changes that would really need to accompany the policy.

Part of the problem is that, even amongst people who support the central idea of the basic income, there are probably very few who could explain the maths or economics that suggest the policy is affordable. But, let's face it, people who do understand the maths and economics involved are probably rather few and far between, whichever side of the argument they support.

Once the above factors have been taken into account, however, it becomes clear that the introduction of a basic income need not cause anything like the financial headaches for the government that many people seem to imagine it would.

In fact, a basic income system, alongside the other changes in taxes and benefits that would naturally accompany its introduction, could easily lead to an improvement in the government's finances - with improved tax revenues and dramatic administrative savings. Certainly, affording a basic income is nothing like the insurmountable problem that some people claim it would be.

Plus, from an Economics perspective - as opposed to a merely financial perspective - there's something even more fundamentally important that should be considered here.

Real economists think, not in terms of money, but in terms of real resources - everything from food to metal ores to people's time. Fundamentally, whether we, as a nation, can 'afford' something, is not really a question of how much money we have. It is a question of whether we have the real resources to achieve our goal. Money is just a way of accounting for those real resources.

And, in terms of real resources, a basic income system doesn't really cost anything at all - because basic income payments (like many other benefit payments) are merely 'transfer payments.' They do not represent the consumption of any additional real resources.

In other words, basic income expenditure is simply money being transferred between people, within the same economy. No new actual goods or real resources are needed in order to be able to afford to provide a basic income.

Basic income payments are provided so that people can feed themselves, clothe themselves, have a home to live in and have enough fuel to keep themselves warm. These are the important real resources that basic income would be paying for. But these resources are already being provided. They're already available!

People already have to be fed, clothed and housed - regardless of how little income they have. Reorganising the financial arrangements associated with these resources doesn't require us to have any extra real resources than we have now. A basic income system does not require us to have any more food, any more clothes, any more houses, or any more fuel than we already have supplied to us. With a basic income, nothing is being

21

fundamentally changed with respect to what resources we have available to us or who will receive those resources. The resources to feed and house people will continue to be distributed to the people (that's everyone) who need to be fed and housed. The main change is simply that the administrative costs of organising this distribution would be dramatically reduced.

So, from an Economics perspective - Economics being about real resources, not money - a basic income is eminently affordable.

Spending money on benefits isn't like spending money on infrastructure projects or on consumer goods imported from China, for example.

If you plan to spend £50 billion on an infrastructure project - then that means you've got to find £50 billion worth of real resources - of raw materials, of machinery, of labour. These resources have to come from somewhere. In fact, they'll probably have to be taken away from other projects that they would otherwise have been used for. We'd have to go without the £50 billion worth of other work they would have been used for if they weren't being engaged on the new infrastructure project.

And if you spend an extra £1 billion on Chinese goods, then you have to pay for those goods. Ultimately, you pay for those goods through exports - by sending to China a billion pounds' worth of your own goods or services - to pay for what you received from China. So, if you can't produce the extra £1 billion in goods or services to send to China, then you can't really afford the extra £1 billion in imports from China.

But benefit payments don't work like that. They merely represent transfer payments between people within your own economy. And, to a large extent, the money is simply being transferred from taxpayers back to those same taxpayers - since every citizen will receive the basic income. Circulating this money in this way just happens to help us efficiently deal with all sorts of poverty-related problems in the process.

Put simply, the idea that a basic income is unaffordable because of the huge sums involved, is really just an illusion. These sums look big in the accounts, but, from an economics perspective, there is no fundamental reason why a basic income scheme would be unaffordable. It isn't unaffordable! There is no fundamental economic barrier to having a basic income system.

But there is one considerable expense to be considered here, that is not merely a series of transfer payments. The very large expense I'm referring to here is the huge cost involved in administrating our current benefit systems.

When tens of thousands of civil servants are paid to run our extensive means-testing systems, their wages and bonuses represent the use - and waste - of very significant and potentially very valuable real resources.

Many millions of man hours are being wasted each year on administrative systems that would not be needed were we to move to a basic income system. Those civil servants - some people might rather disparagingly refer to them as bureaucrats - will include many educated and skilled people. These are people whose sometimes rather substantial abilities could be put to vastly more productive use, if they weren't being wasted on unnecessary bureaucratic procedures. Let's stop wasting these valuable people's time and energy on pointless bureaucracy!

23

So, in every important sense - in fundamental economic terms, in terms of real resources - a basic income would be substantially cheaper than our current tax and benefit system.

I'll stress this again: A basic income does not require us to have any more resources than we have now. It is a policy that affects how resources are distributed and accounted for, but it does not require us to have any additional resources.

Indeed, it requires fewer resources. It frees up thousands of government workers to go and do other, more productive work, instead of being tied up in the wasteful means-testing bureaucracy we currently burden ourselves with. And it frees millions of workers or other claimants from that bureaucracy too.

So, is it affordable? Overwhelmingly, yes. Indeed, the more sensible question would be whether we can afford to continue with the bureaucratic, inefficient, complicated mess of a tax and benefits system that we currently endure.

Millionaires

One of the other headline criticisms of basic income is that it would involve paying benefits to millionaires. And it is true - it would (unless they refuse to accept them - which many probably would do).

The problem is that many people seem to instinctively react against the idea of benefits for millionaires and fail to examine the issue more carefully and more intelligently. The idea of millionaires getting benefits is so abhorrent to them, that the basic income is almost instantly dismissed as an outright silly idea - but, of course, it shouldn't be!

It should only take a moment to realise that it doesn't matter if millionaires receive benefits - so long as that extra money is paid back by them through their taxes. What counts is their net contribution. If a millionaire gets a few thousand a year in basic income payments, but pays a vastly larger sum in taxes, then what is the problem? There isn't one. It doesn't matter that they will receive the basic income - because they will be paying much, much more than that in tax.

The only actual problem might be if there were high administrative costs involved in taxing millionaires and then paying them a small fraction of that money back. One might instinctively assume that paying millionaires benefits and then taxing them more to pay for it will be more complicated and more costly than our current system - but that really isn't the case.

In fact, the opposite would be true. If every citizen is entitled to exactly the same basic income, then the system requires very little administration at all. You simply need to verify that a person is a citizen and get their bank account details - and then you just need to be informed if they die or leave the country.

Thanks to the beautiful simplicity of the basic income system, taxing millionaires and then paying them a small amount back in basic income payments is actually much more efficient than our current tax and benefit system - because no means-testing will be involved.

Sure, the millionaires themselves are unlikely to be means-tested under our current system - because they probably won't be claiming those sorts of benefits. But, millions of other claimants have to be means-tested in order to distinguish them from the millionaires and other relatively well-off people. With a basic income system, none of that means-testing is necessary any more - and we save billions as a result!

The whole complaint of millionaires receiving benefits is really just a silly red herring that relies on people being gullible and too lazy to think the situation through for themselves. It is a scare story that we have no need to be scared by, if we just think about it for one minute.

Incentives

Well, suppose we accept then, that a basic income is eminently affordable? Many other benefits will no longer be needed, tax allowances will no longer be needed, pension tax relief can be scaled back, income tax can be moderately raised and we would seem to be able to pay for the new system without any major difficulties. And the criticism that it will involve benefits being paid to millionaires is a huge red herring.

But now we must deal with another possible concern: How will a basic income affect the key incentives that are fundamental to the way our economy operates?

The fear that fuels some of the most prominent criticism of the basic income is that a basic income would hugely undermine or even destroy the incentive systems on which our incomes and wealth rely.

Some people, including some people who instinctively like the essential idea of a basic income, are genuinely concerned that there may be hundreds of thousands or even millions of people who decide they will no longer make any attempt to look for and find jobs and will, instead, be happy to live on their basic income alone.

In the nightmare scenario, the economy would shrink as millions decide to stop working altogether. One of the results of this might be that tax receipts would fall dramatically, lead to a massive budget deficit for the government - and potential financial collapse if the situation continued unabated.

Fortunately, whilst this fear of widespread

fecklessness is regularly encouraged by some politicians and several national newspapers, there is no need to panic, because, in truth, such fears have little if any basis in economic reality. Indeed, they seem decidedly at odds with the available evidence of how all but a few people actually behave.

When you think about it, how many people would really be so reluctant to work that they would go without everything other than absolute essentials? 'Hardly anyone' is the answer - an answer squarely backed up by mountains of economic data.

It is a question of understanding human psychology. Will there be some people who try to live entirely on their basic income and make no effort to find additional work to boost their incomes? Yes, there will be some - but a relatively tiny number. Most people are just not like that - just look around you!

The vast majority of people are not satisfied with the essentials. They're not satisfied with having enough to eat and with entertaining themselves by reading books from the library. They want a car. They want an expensive smartphone and a contract with a generous phone call, text and data allowance. They want satellite or cable TV. They want games consoles and the latest games. They want to eat out in restaurants. They want takeaways. They enjoy a drink. They want holidays abroad. They want concert tickets. And the basic income is not going to provide these things!

So seriously, what percentage of the population will actually be happy to go without any of these things (or other luxuries) and make do with only the essentials and whatever they can get their hands on or do for free?

Millions of people already spend long hours at work, for low pay, in jobs they dislike - so that they can have the far-from-necessary extras that, for whatever reason, they decide they really don't want to live without. What reasons have we to think that a basic income would change this basic situation in any substantial way? None, really!

Some people really have become ridiculously obsessed by the popular notion of the benefits scrounger. The archetypal benefits scrounger is portrayed by certain sections of the media as a feckless layabout who still manages to get enough in benefits to pay for their cigarettes, alcohol, lottery tickets and large-screen TV, claiming every benefit under the sun they can possibly get their hands on and exaggerating their needs at every opportunity.

This narrative of countless feckless, work-shy people has, at best, only a very tenuous relationship to reality. Such people do exist - though in much more limited numbers than some newspapers would have us believe - but these people might well end up with rather less under a basic income system than they get now. And who amongst even them will be willing to go without their cigarettes or alcohol or iphone or other luxuries?

And the fraudsters? The simplicity of the basic income would make fraud more difficult - and much easier to investigate, easier to detect and easier to prove if discovered.

In all probability, under a basic income system, the vast majority of people will continue to work just as they do today.

Even those who do try to live entirely off their basic income, are not, on the whole going to be lazy or feckless people. Most of them will be making a contribution in ways other than through formal work. They may be mothers (or fathers) looking after children. They may be carers, looking after the disabled or the old and infirm. They may be artistic types or intellectuals, for whom material goods have little appeal, but who still contribute to society in their own ways.

On the whole, a basic income system is highly likely to improve the work incentives in our economy.

Currently, many people are disincentivised to work, because, if they find work or get themselves more work, they will be penalised through loss of benefits. Some people will argue that they should take work anyway, since they should (for some reason) be ashamed to accept benefits. But who amongst such critics can honestly say they themselves would readily accept a job when doing so might make them and their children worse off?

The withdrawal of benefits when people find work or increase their work hours, does create a powerful and harmful disincentive to find work. A basic income system, however, removes such harmful disincentives - and by doing so it might well reduce worklessness, not increase it.

The people who claim a basic income would undermine the work ethic are probably largely from the same group of people who complain that our current benefits system undermines the work ethic and who complain that the benefits regime should be harsher on the unemployed in order to push them into work. But such people should probably be welcoming the idea of a basic income - because it might well do far more to entice people into work than any of the harsh benefit sanctions or other measures they might well be in favour of.

There are people who are very much willing to work, but who are reluctant to work in jobs they dislike, for employers who would treat them badly. A basic income might mean employers have to work harder to entice people to work for them - but that's probably rather a good thing. Businesses should be there to serve people - not the other way around.

With very few exceptions, people who are used to working aren't suddenly going to stop as a result of getting the basic income. People are creatures of habit. They'll carry on pretty much as they do now. And the economy as a whole will continue to operate, under a basic income system, pretty much the same way it does now. The basic income is not at all likely to bring about the economic apocalypse.

And basic income could also improve other positive incentives in our economy and reduce harmful incentives. For example, consider the incentives around savings. Saving plays an important role in our economies. Anyone with money has, in effect, control over important real resources. By spending their money on wasteful consumer goods, they are directing real and valuable resources towards the production of those consumer goods.

On the other hand, by saving, not only are they 'investing' in financial terms, but they are allowing real resources to be directed towards investing for the future rather than for present day consumption.

I won't go into all the details here, but the point is that saving plays an important role in directing real resources towards investment - such as conducting important research or building the factories, housing and infrastructure of the future - rather than towards wasteful consumption. Saving helps secure a more prosperous future - for the economy as a whole, not just for the individual savers in question.

Unfortunately, our current benefits system often heavily discourages saving. If you save instead of wasting your money on cigarettes, excessive alcohol or lottery tickets, you may well get penalised by missing out on benefits.

The conscientious worker who saves into a savings account in case she loses her job, may make herself ineligible for means-tested benefits if she does lose her job. The reckless worker who does not save any of his income, is rewarded with benefits that the conscientious saver is denied. This isn't fair. It also discourages saving, when saving is something the government ought to be encouraging.

These perverse disincentives to save are the result of the means-testing nature of our existing benefits regime. With a basic income, these damaging disincentives disappear.

Poverty is linked to a lack of savings - for some obvious reasons and for some less obvious ones. Obviously, people who live in poverty may be not be able to afford to save money. But things can work the other way around too; a lack of savings can contribute very considerably to poverty, by causing people to have to spend more than they otherwise would.

Savings allow you to spend more effectively. They provide a means through which you can switch your spending to times when it provides the most benefit - when you can get the best deal.

Savings allow people to 'invest' in items that help

save them money. For example, someone with savings can buy a washing machine, instead of having to go to a launderette - saving huge amounts on their annual laundry bill. People without savings could probably still buy a washing machine - but might well be doing so through taking out credit and paying excessive interest payments in the process.

People without savings are often taken advantage of - whether it be through consumer credit deals or expensive pay-as-you-go electricity meters. They don't have access to the best deals.

So, allowing and encouraging people to have savings is a key part of any sensible anti-poverty strategy - yet our means-testing benefits regime actually discourages savings. What sense could it possibly make to do this?

With a basic income system, people will be free to work and free to save, without having to worry about the effect of extra income or extra savings on their benefits.

So, contrary to what many people might assume, a basic income may well radically improve incentives in our economy. It is very likely to encourage people to work, not discourage them. It may well lead to fewer workless households, not more. And it may boost incentives to save and incentives to invest.

Arguments that it is likely to harm incentives just don't hold much water when examined in the light of the available evidence about how most people are known to behave.

And basic income could improve incentives in more subtle ways. It gives us each the opportunity and the incentive to find more worthwhile work, to consider more options, to reassess our careers and our lives and make better long-term choices. Faced with choices, rather than obligations, we can steer own own lives and the economy as a whole into a more productive, more worthwhile direction for the future.

Wages

Another important thing that will have to be considered before the basic income is introduced, is how wages would be affected. Is it possible, for example, that the basic income will lead to a fall in people's wages?

We will also have to decide what should happen with regard to the minimum wage. Will we still need a minimum wage? If we continue to have one, should the level of the minimum wage be adjusted?

It is possible that a basic income could lead to a reduction in wages for some people - for simple demand and supply reasons. If people have the security of a basic income, they don't need as much money in wages as they used to need. They can afford - and may be willing - to work for less. The demand and supply situation has changed - and so some changes to wage levels might occur.

But the risks of lower wages can easily be overstated. Suppose that basic income is set at £80 a week. Well, for a person in a full-time job, who works 40 hours per week, that basic income is only £2 per hour that they work.

So, it is possible that instead of someone earning £10 an hour, they might receive their basic income, but then only be paid £8 an hour in wages. Ultimately, they have the same income at the end of the week. It is just that instead of the business paying its workers £10 an hour, they pay a little extra in taxes, which gets paid to their workers in basic income. They still pay most of the employees' money to them directly as wages.

That wouldn't be a drastic change. In fact,

however, changes are likely to be much smaller even than that - for the simple reason that basic income is essentially a replacement benefit, not an additional benefit on top of the benefits we already have. It would be replacing a lot of existing benefits - and changing one system of benefits for another does not necessarily impose any downward pressure on wages.

Our benefits system is already subsidising wages. It just does so in a very uneven, hit and miss, haphazard fashion. The basic income would be much fairer - the 'subsidy' would be evenly spread across the whole population. And, of course, the employers still ultimately have to foot the bill through taxation - just as they do now for existing benefits. So, in this sense, the basic income is not likely to bring about any sudden, traumatic changes in the labour market, as some people might fear.

And when you take into account the fact that basic income payments will be offset by changes in tax allowances, there's even more reason to think that the basic income will not undermine wage levels.

In fact, there are clear reasons to believe that the basic income might very well help raise wages. For one thing, it fundamentally improves the bargaining position of employees. It means they are no longer forced to work in order to pay for essentials, and so are in a much stronger position to strike a fair deal with employers.

In terms of negotiating power, it puts the boot on the other foot, because the potential employee can say to an employer, 'No, I don't have to work for you. If you want me to do that job, you're going to have to make it worth my while.' It means employers may have to rely rather more on the carrot and rather less heavily on the stick.

It may be that some employers may be able to pay workers less as a result of the introduction of a basic income. This might especially be the case if they have no problem enticing people to work for them, if the job is a good one - enjoyable, pleasant - and if they treat their workers well. In such circumstances, competition amongst workers to secure such a job might lead to a reduction in the market wage.

On the other hand, many employers wanting people to do less pleasant jobs, who perhaps don't treat their workers especially well, may have to pay more than they do now. Because the basic income would mean no-one *has* to work for them, they may have to do more to incentivise people to work for them anyway - and this may well mean higher wages and better working conditions than at present.

And, in the longer term, the basic income may have an even more fundamental influence on helping people to earn higher wages. The basic income will give people more freedom to take breaks from working full-time in order to further educate themselves or take up training opportunities. They could develop the skills to make themselves more productive in future, thus boosting their ability to command higher wages. In this way, the basic income could help us develop the high-skill, high-wage economy of the future.

So, in all likelihood, the basic income, rather than precipitating any sudden or traumatic changes, would produce a gentle but very important change in emphasis in the labour market - a change in emphasis that boosts the position and status of ordinary workers.

The onus would be on employers to provide jobs that people want to do - or at least to reward them well for doing jobs they don't especially enjoy. Employers will no longer be able to rely on people's need to take some sort of job, however unpleasant it might be or however poorly their employer treats them.

Rather than the emphasis being on people having to compete against each other for work, businesses have to compete against each other to convince people to work for them. To be successful, businesses will have to come up with a package of benefits that entices people to accept a particular job.

It means that the emphasis will be on businesses serving people, instead of people having to serve businesses. That sounds to me like a fantastic change for the better!

So, what about the minimum wage?

Well, one particularly appealing feature of the basic income is that it would free people from the obligations of having to work and give them more freedom to work doing what they want to do.

In such circumstances, it would be nice for people, with the security of the basic income behind them, to have the option of working for less than the current minimum wage, if that allowed them to do a job they would particularly enjoy, gain experience they feel is important, pursue a career they really wanted to pursue and/or do work they really thought would make a valuable contribution to society.

The basic income would take care of their essential needs and, whilst they might want to earn some extra money, their chief concern might be to do work they would enjoy doing and which they feel is particularly worthwhile, rather than to earn as much as possible.

Unfortunately, sometimes, the particular work they might especially want to do, might not be especially profitable and it genuinely might not be realistically possible for an employer to pay them minimum wage and still make a profit out of that activity. And the higher the minimum wage is, the more likely it is that minimum wage rules could interfere with people's freedom to do the jobs they want to do.

Minimum wage rules are there to stop people being exploited by employers. But, with a basic income giving people more negotiating power in the labour market, we might no longer need the minimum wage. The basic income could take over the job of protecting people from exploitation. And it could do so in a way that doesn't restrict people's job options in the way that the minimum wage sometimes does.

So, the introduction of the basic income might well lead us to conclude that the minimum wage should be lowered. It is entirely possible that we might ultimately consider it no longer necessary or desirable to have a minimum wage at all. We want to give people the freedom to do the jobs they really want to do, rather than being restricted to only those jobs that can pay the minimum wage.

Nevertheless, it might be a good idea, at the launch of a basic income, to maintain the minimum wage. This would help to minimise potential transitional problems - or transitional concerns - as the economy adjusts to a basic income system.

Any relaxation of minimum wage rules could be brought in at a later date, once it has been clearly established that a basic income system does not necessitate any dramatic changes in wage levels.

Pensions

A basic income system is likely to be accompanied by changes in our pension system.

This is primarily because it would seem somewhat ludicrous and unfair to have a non-means-tested basic income for working age adults, but to still have means-testing for pensioners. And if we seek the enormous benefits of reduced administration costs and hassles for working age benefits, why not seek the same benefits with regard to pensions?

So, alongside the introduction of a basic income for working-age people, it would seem eminently sensible to have a non-means-tested basic income for pensioners too. It would operate on exactly the same principles as the basic income - and might well be referred to as the Basic Pension. In all probability, however, it will be significantly more than the basic income paid to other adults.

But why would we pay a higher rate of basic income to pensioners? Well, the basic income for working-age adults would probably be substantially less than the current full state pension. This is because the basic income is meant to be set at a subsistence level - sufficient to pay for essentials, but little else. People who want more then have the incentive to work in order to earn more.

A pension, on the other hand, should be set higher than a subsistence level. It is supposed to provide for more than just the absolute essentials. It is supposed to provide some sort of reward for a lifetime's work.

Now, of course, many people will be receiving some form of occupational or private pension - and, in time, it may become standard practice to consider that the government should just provide a standard basic income to everyone and leave it to individuals to arrange any additional pension provision they may wish to have.

But, as things stand, there are many people approaching retirement who will be largely relying on a state pension and, after a lifetime of paying their taxes and national insurance, quite rightly expect the state pension to be sufficient to pay for a reasonable lifestyle - not just for bare essentials.

So, on the introduction of a basic income, the basic income for pensioners (the basic pension) should be higher than it is for other people.

Furthermore, some people have been making sacrifices over many years in order to make additional pension payments - sometimes through voluntary contributions - in expectation of qualifying for a more generous state pension. It is reasonable to ensure that these people are rewarded for their responsible actions - and receive some degree of top-up to the Basic Pension.

In decades to come, this top-up system should no longer be needed, as additional pension provision could by then be regarded as a private matter and no business of the state. The state role will be simply to deliver the Basic Pension, ensuring no-one need go without essentials.

The change to a basic pension should bring about vast administrative savings. For one thing, the central reason for having national insurance in addition to income tax will have disappeared. The introduction of a basic income would therefore provide an excellent opportunity to scrap national insurance and simply combine it into a higher rate of income tax, which would be much easier to understand.

This change will also allow us to save significant amounts in administration costs. We will be able to do without all the worry and administrative expense of collecting different forms of national insurance and deciding when those payments do or do not qualify a person for a credit for that particular year.

A Basic Pension would give people much more than just money. It would give them financial security and peace of mind. Every citizen will know that they will have a sufficient pension when they reach pensionable age. No means-testing, no worrying about national insurance qualifying years or credits - just straightforward, reliable, stress-free pension provision for every citizen.

It is something every rich, developed economy ought to provide - but which many, strangely, don't. Really, there's no excuse for it!

One instinctive concern might be with regard to people who already have generous private or occupational pension provision. Wouldn't it be wasteful to give a basic pension to such people who are already so very well off?

But that concern has already been taken care of, of course, as tax changes, including the removal of personal tax allowances, would mean they would pay more tax on those other pensions. Thus, most of the basic pension payments made to such people would be paid back through tax.

The simplicity of the basic income system helps solve all sorts of problems. Even possible drawbacks seem to come with simple, natural solutions.

Ah, but what about incentives? Currently, people may be incentivised to work - or work harder - in order to be able to afford pension payments and be able to provide for their retirement. Wouldn't a guaranteed, non-means-tested pension for every citizen undermine such incentives?

Well, no - not to any noticeable degree. In fact, such incentives may be improved by the basic income and basic pension.

People work for all manner of things they wouldn't otherwise be able to afford. They work chiefly to have things long before their pension. They work so they can go for a night out at the weekend. They work to be able to afford a beer or a packet of cigarettes or a decent holiday or a new car.

Some people do work with their retirement prospects in mind, but whilst the basic pension will provide an income above subsistence levels, it will still be less than most people would reasonably aspire to.

So, most people will still prefer to have some sort of extra pension provision in addition to the basic pension. They won't *need* it, but most people will still be prepared to work a little harder during their working lives in order to be able to make that additional pension provision.

In fact, knowing that extra work and extra saving will indeed provide extra income in retirement, could greatly boost work incentives. At present, many people are in a very uncertain position regarding their pension provision. They want to have a comfortable retirement, but they know their own private pension provision may make them ineligible for means-tested state pension payments when they retire - and this may discourage them from making any private pension provision at all.

Someone paying nothing into a pension scheme will still be able to get the pension credit to bring their income up to the government-determined minimum level. However, someone who spends years or decades paying into a pension scheme may find that most or even all of that extra saving is effectively stolen off them when they retire, because for every pound they receive from their own private or occupational pension scheme, they lose a pound in means-tested pension credit.

This ridiculous system seems grossly unfair and severely disincentivises people to save for a pension. A basic income and basic pension scheme, however, would zap this problem into non-existence.

So, in additional to all the other problems it helps with - tackling poverty and reducing bureaucracy and improving work incentives - a basic income system could revolutionise, for the better, our complicated and antiquated system of pension provision. The basic income just seems to appear more and more attractive the more you think about it!

Housing

In considering what level basic income should be set at, one major area of debate would be with regard to whether the basic income should cover housing costs.

If it doesn't - if we say that basic income is not supposed to cover housing costs - you're left with people having to apply for separate housing benefits. This would probably involve means-testing and would thus partially undermine a key purpose of having the basic income in the first place, as means-testing is obviously a major part of what a basic income system seeks to avoid.

But if basic income is supposed to cover housing costs, potential problems emerge because housing costs vary so significantly from one part of the country to another.

If we pay everyone enough to be able to afford to live in the most expensive parts of the country, then a basic income would indeed become unaffordable. Besides which, you'll be paying most people vastly more than they need to live on - so much that people really might have a dramatically reduced incentive to find work - so that really isn't an option.

So what can we do? We could have different levels of basic income in different parts of the country - to reflect the widely differing costs of housing. That, though, would undermine the simplicity of the basic income system. It would also seem unfair in many ways.

This whole problem, though, is not specifically related to basic income at all. The problem of how to deal with divergent housing costs is one that has made benefit policy difficult for a long time.

Should we really pay someone more benefit just so they can live in an expensive part of London - or should they simply have to move to a cheaper area? Why should taxpayers pay for people to be able to live in an expensive area - when most of those taxpayers couldn't afford to live there themselves?

But, on the other hand, suppose someone is unemployed or disabled and happens to come from an expensive part of the country. If we refuse to pay them housing benefits sufficient to pay for local housing, then we might be effectively forcing them away from the place they call home - away from friends and family. Is that reasonable or is it cruel?

Historically, through housing benefit, we have paid more in benefits to people living in expensive areas - but perhaps this whole situation needs rethinking.

If we stopped doing this, then people who did not have well-paid jobs would usually need to move to cheaper areas of the country, where housing is more plentiful and cheaper.

If this means that there is a shortage of available workers in those expensive areas of the country - if schools there are short of teachers, hospitals are short of nurses and almost everyone is crying out for more cleaners - then perhaps the exorbitant house prices there will come down. Perhaps that's just the market doing its job.

Most people in the UK can't really afford to live in London - not in any reasonably-sized or reasonably-maintained accommodation anyway. And people who don't live in expensive parts of the country shouldn't really be asked to subsidise those who do.

I think the basic income should cover basic housing costs. After all, people have to live somewhere, no matter how well or poorly paid they are. It doesn't, however, have to cover anything more than the basics.

A modest amount to cover housing costs will encourage people to share, to pool their resources, to make more efficient use of the available housing stock. And yes, if people find that the basic income is insufficient to cover their housing costs in an expensive part of the country, then I think they should be prepared to move elsewhere.

If people have friends and family members in the area who they would like to stay close to, then perhaps those friends and family will be willing to offer them a room or to assist them with their housing costs.

If friends and family can barely afford to live there themselves, then they can, if they wish, all decide to move elsewhere in the country. The basic income would give them the freedom to do that. It would cover their basic living costs in the cheaper parts of the country, affording them all as much time as they need to find new jobs for themselves without the fear of having nothing to live on in the meantime.

And if expensive areas of the country need more workers, then it is down to the people and businesses and local authorities in those areas to provide affordable accommodation for those workers - to attract people to move there and look for work there.

Paying extra in benefits to people in London, so that we can have low-paid workers in London, is basically just an exercise in subsidising the rich -

so that there are still staff available to work for low wages in the local shops and restaurants. The extra benefits may be paid to the poor, but they are primarily for the benefit of the rich. This is an absurd system that is well overdue a serious rethink.

If local authorities along with local businesses or other organisations in the more expensive parts of the country want to run schemes to help provide cheap or subsidised housing for lower-paid workers and thus help to retain such workers in their particular area, then that is down to them. It shouldn't be up to taxpayers in the rest of the country to subsidise such schemes.

I think some government role in guaranteeing the availability of housing will be required, however. If the basic income only covers the most basic level of accommodation, it could be difficult for some people to get any sort of accommodation.

Some people will be able to secure reasonable accommodation through cooperation - by pooling their money with others to jointly rent a reasonably decent property. Others, however, lacking friends or family members to cooperate with, won't be able to do this.

I think it is incredibly important that no-one should be homeless, so I think there should be some form of government guarantee with regard to basic housing. It should guarantee to provide anyone with some reasonable, but basic form of accommodation in return for a fixed, affordable proportion of their basic income each week - an amount that still leaves them sufficient money to pay for food and other essentials.

That accommodation might only be a small room or, for single people, just a decent dormitory bed in a basic, but clean hostel - but nobody in a modern, developed economy, should be homeless. We simply have no reasonable excuse whatsoever to tolerate people having to live on the streets.

A basic income should cover a person's essential needs - and accommodation of some sort is clearly a pretty essential need. In some countries, where the climate is warmer, it might not be, but in the UK, accommodation is essential.

Other Issues

There are other issues to consider. For example; won't a basic income encourage excessive immigration - attracting migrants with a no-questions-asked weekly payment?

Well, we need firstly to bear in mind, again, that basic income will be paid *instead* of many existing benefits, not in addition to them. If migrants were paid basic income - and they might well not be - you have to take into consideration that, whilst they may gain from that, they might well be losing out in terms of the many discontinued benefits that they might currently be entitled to. Furthermore, their tax rates would be higher in order to help pay for the basic income. It is not certain, therefore, that the overall incentive for immigration would be higher than it is now.

And it may well be, in any case, that the basic income is restricted, quite strictly, to full citizens and not available to migrants from other countries.

In the case of the UK, however, this might cause problems. If eligibility for basic income payments were restricted to full UK citizens, it might be claimed that this discriminates against other EU citizens. It might therefore conflict with European Union rules.

If that is the case, then I think there are some clear possible solutions. One possibility is to push for all EU countries to introduce a basic income, so as to lessen the incentive for people to migrate for benefit reasons. If other EU member states are really our partners and are genuinely interested in the common good, then they may support such a move.

Otherwise, it is simply a matter of asserting sovereignty. If EU rules conflicted with the introduction of a basic income, then EU rules would simply have to change. If other EU members refused to accommodate that, then we can simply leave the EU.

Many millions of people already think that we would be better off outside the EU - but, even if we believe that we benefit from EU membership, the benefits might be quite small in comparison to the huge and obvious benefits of having a basic income system. If the EU acts as a barrier to the basic income, then even otherwise pro-EU people might consider that too high a price to pay for EU membership.

In the UK, in recent years, basic income has received support, both from UKIP, who fiercely oppose EU membership and from the Green Party, who are generally in favour of EU membership. These parties tend to disagree on many other issues. The basic income is such an important idea, however, that we shouldn't let it be derailed, either by the EU or by differences of opinion about the EU.

Basic income makes incredible sense. It promises enormous benefits. Basic income is, very likely, the future - but whether or not the EU is part of the future may depend on how supportive it is of brilliant ideas such as the basic income - a real and powerful solution to so many problems common to many European countries.

In Context

To fully understand the rationale for the basic income, it is important to put our current economic situation in a broad, historical context.

Once, human beings were hunter-gatherers. Our economy consisted largely of activities designed to harvest the bounty of nature.

Then, we became primarily farmers - planting crops for ourselves. And, over the centuries, we became pretty good at it. In particular; prior to and alongside the industrial revolution (here in Britain), an agricultural revolution saw huge increases in farming efficiency and in food production. This freed up labour to work in the newly-emerging factories and fuelled the industrial revolution.

Then, in the modern era, advanced mass-production and automation have meant a reduction in the need for industrial workers - and have freed up labour to work in the service sector.

Potentially, we have a new revolution in the offing. Information technology, in the form of computers and other electronic devices, raises the potential (though so far, often unrealised) to provide services much more efficiently.

But what next? What happens if we do successfully manage to provide services much more efficiently? Once we have all the goods and materials and manufactured goods and services we need, once we have all we could reasonably use or consume and are prepared to pay for, what will we do then?

Well, the common, rarely questioned assumption at the heart of most governments' economic policies is that we will simply continue to consume more and more with no limit. However much we think we may need or want, our governments believe we can be persuaded to want even more. This seems to be what governments are relying on to deliver what they assume to be 'economic success.' Economic growth without end is what they seem to be seeking - with people producing, buying and consuming ever larger quantities of produce, goods and services.

But aren't they just ignoring what ought to be obvious; that such a situation, even if it were possible, would not be remotely desirable? It isn't going to be good for us or for the health of the planet we live on.

The dream of simply consuming more and more without end is an empty and mindless dream that is only likely to result in disaster. Beyond a certain point, more consumption doesn't, on the whole, make us better off. In fact, it often makes us worse off and destroys our environment in the process. It isn't going to work.

So, what alternatives are there to an economy of ever-increasing production and consumption?

It was once a popular idea to look forward to the life of leisure. Indeed, it was once a widespread expectation that we would already be living the life of leisure by now; all the hard work done by machines and computers, with humans providing the necessary creative inputs, but having most of their time free to use as they please.

Some people would just concentrate on enjoying themselves. Others, however, freed from labour, would be able to bend their efforts to scientific or cultural pursuits, as they see fit.

It seems like a perfectly good aspiration; a future where humans are freed from want and enabled, through technology and productive efficiency, to choose how to spend their lives and choose what dreams to pursue. But, on the whole, we're not living the life of leisure. Indeed, working hours may even be getting longer.

Perhaps part of the problem is that we just haven't worked out how our society should be organised when it is no longer necessary or beneficial or desirable for everyone to be fully employed.

Already, we have the technology - provided we utilise it effectively - to provide all the food, manufactured goods and services we could ever reasonably demand, using only a fraction of the available labour force.

But this situation raises some weighty, unanswered questions. What is all this freed labour going to do? When we can meet all our needs, still leaving millions of unneeded workers, how should our society then be organised so that we can avoid people going without food or other essentials? If there is a lack of work to go round, how can we fairly distribute the work that we have and the resources we control? Such questions have been looming over our societies for some time, with surprisingly little effort by politicians to address them.

It is not that we need our 'spare workers' to do anything, as we would already be providing all the goods and services sufficient to meet everyone's needs - but we do need a way to achieve a reasonable distribution of wealth, so that no-one need go without.

Suppose we could meet all our needs and wants using only half the available workforce. We could have a situation where half the labour force is well-off and in work and the other half is unemployed and in poverty.

One solution would be to try to redistribute work, so the work is spread more evenly - perhaps with almost every available worker being employed, but only working part time. A tax system could be devised to give companies an incentive to employ more part-time workers instead of a more limited number of full-time workers. For example, wages on the first 20 hours of work a week could be taxed at a lower rate than those for additional hours. But that might be inefficient in many ways - e.g. having to train two part-time workers instead of one full-time worker.

And, in practice, some people will want to work full-time, whilst others would be happier working far fewer hours. Some people's lives revolve around their careers and they genuinely want to work fairly long hours. Other people might want to make a full and worthwhile contribution to society, but through means other than those that provide a commercial return. Full-time mothers is an obvious example.

The basic income is an idea that looks forward in a positive way to a more efficient, more enlightened future society - a society no longer obsessed with excessive consumption, in which we simply do not need or desire the sheer quantity of goods and resources that we could supply if everyone worked full-time. In this future society, many people would still work, but that would be through choice. People would be freed from the obligation to work - and certainly from any obligation to work long hours.

Before we can develop this advanced future society, however, there will be a long transitional period to go through, in which we still need millions of workers, but in which we have more labour than we need. A basic income could be a very important way of helping us manage this transitional period. Indeed, it could be a way in which a more futuristic economy and more enlightened society could be encouraged to develop.

As things are, we seem to be largely rudderless - with little thought being given to the direction our societies should be heading in - or how our future societies should be organised.

We're not sure we can keep everyone employed full-time - or how that could be a good thing, even if we could. If improved productivity were to free up labour, we don't seem to have any plan as to what we will do with that freed labour - or how we could organise a reasonable distribution of income and wealth when work is scarce.

Indeed, it is entirely possible that our lack of ideas in this respect may actually be contributing to our severe lack of progress in terms of increasing productivity and providing services more efficiently. We just wouldn't know what to do with all our spare labour, with all those no-longer-needed working hours if we did do things more efficiently.

We imagine we need people to keep working so that they can continue to afford to buy the enormous quantities of goods and services we keep producing - even though we are already producing far more than we really need and far more than is good for us.

Instead of organising ourselves more efficiently and reaping the benefits of shorter working hours, we end up mindlessly producing and consuming ever greater quantities of goods and services we don't really benefit from. It is not so much that we are entirely bereft of ideas about where our economy should be heading next. It is more that we are too timid, too lacking in confidence to embrace or even fully explore the ideas that are offered.

If we consider the situation at all intelligently, we'll probably conclude that there could be a brighter future beyond the mindless pursuit of consumption for consumption's sake. We just need to stop being afraid of it!

Ethics

The debate on basic income is sometimes hindered by some rather ill-considered ideas of ethics or morality.

There are people who will argue - or, more frequently, just strongly imply - that there is something morally dubious about receiving benefits. You get these comments about people 'living off the state' - as if there is something fundamentally immoral about receiving benefits.

In the general case, this is nonsense. The state taxes people and a fraction of that money is paid out in benefit payments.

People pay taxes when they receive a decent income. They pay taxes when they spend that income. They can't refuse to pay their taxes. So, when they are are on low income and benefits become available to them, why should they refuse to accept them?

Ah - but what about those who receive more in benefits than they pay in taxes? Well, it is perfectly reasonable that there should be many such people. The general principle in operation is that the tax people pay should be related to their ability to pay, whereas benefits should be paid to those in need - and, obviously, people's needs and their ability to pay do not always match.

The basic income still operates according to these basic principles, but simplifies the administration involved. Instead of having to assess people for their ability to pay and also assessing them for their needs, it simply recognises that everyone has needs - and nearly everyone has essentially the same basic needs - the need to eat, the need for shelter. So really, it is only people's ability to pay that we actually need to assess - and we do that through the tax system.

So let's get over the silly idea that there is something fundamentally immoral about receiving benefits.

Of course, there are some people who abuse the system. They seek to live at other people's expense and avoid making much of a contribution themselves - in the form of paid work, for example. But the numbers of such people are probably far lower than many people - under the influence of some notoriously biased newspapers - tend to believe.

The focus by some parts of the media and some unscrupulous politicians on alleged 'benefit scroungers' is really very childish - and, frankly, rather nasty. The overwhelming evidence is that, with very few exceptions, people will happily work hard if they get the opportunity to do so, if they are reasonably rewarded for doing so and if they are treated well by their employers.

In any case, people who are worried about benefits scroungers should probably support the idea of the basic income - because it takes away major disincentives that might dissuade benefit recipients from finding work. It dramatically improves people's incentive to make a worthwhile contribution to the society they live in - something people of almost all political persuasions really ought to welcome.

And then there's something much more fundamental that we ought to consider here. Some people complain about benefit recipients and deride some of them as people who 'think the state owes them a living.' But really, the state does owe each of us quite a bit.

Historically, people used to be able to make a living from the land. They were free to harvest the bounty of nature. They went foraging. They hunted. They went fishing. They planted their own crops. They grazed animals on common land. They chopped wood in the forest.

It was the state that took away our freedoms to support ourselves in these traditional ways. It allowed and encouraged land to be sectioned off and divided amongst a relatively small section of society. A small number of people become wealthy landowners. Almost everyone else was demoted to being dependent on those wealthy landowners for access to the land and to the food supply.

Wealth continues to be concentrated in the hands of a relatively small number of people. The state, through its laws, police, courts and officials, supports this status quo - even though the uneven distribution of wealth is largely an accident of history, rather than any sort of fair reflection of merit.

There are understandable reasons why the state acts as it does in respect of protecting property rights. Most ordinary people want stability - and so does the state.

Nevertheless, it is the state that denies people the right to farm the land, grow crops and raise animals - unless, that is, you own land that very few can afford. So, in return, doesn't it have a clear moral duty to provide everyone with the means to live by? Isn't that the least we ought to be able to demand, given that our natural freedom to live off the land has been taken away from us?

We ought to stop acting as if the state is doing us a favour whenever it hands out modest amounts in benefit payments.

The state should be there to serve us. We're the ones who are doing the state a favour - by allowing it to exist, by allowing our lands and properties and incomes to be taxed, by allowing our lives to be restricted by state laws and regulations and state-appointed officials.

We don't owe the state anything. Everything the state owns, we own. We should have the right to tell the state what to do with its property, its assets, its tax revenues - because that is our property and those are our assets and our tax revenues.

The right to make your own living was taken away by the state. Today, people have to rely on employers. The employer decides whether to offer you a living - you cannot make them do so. Even if you are self-employed, you rely on customers. You cannot make people buy your products, even if your products are far superior to those available elsewhere. There is no fundamental right to earn your own living, as there used to be.

It can, of course, be argued that the development of the modern state and the privatisation of most land and other property is, on the whole, beneficial. But, by denying people the right to live off the land, the state picks up a responsibility to those people - a responsibility to provide for their basic needs. A basic income could help the state fulfil its moral obligations and meet that responsibility.

A New Philosophy

It's time to get philosophical.

It should be clear to anyone with a reasonable understanding of Economics, who has actually studied the issue in any depth, that a basic income system has enormous potential to provide great practical benefits - practical benefits in terms of dramatically simplifying our tax and benefit system and greatly reducing the very significant administration costs involved - costs that ultimately have to be paid for by taxpayers.

For some people, their great enthusiasm for the basic income stems largely from these practical advantages. They can see the realistic prospect of saving tens of billions of pounds every year - and, more importantly, the real resources those billions represent. A monumental reduction in bureaucratic waste is in the offing - and they're very enthusiastic about taking up that offer.

However, there's much more to the basic income than such practical benefits. It's not just about freeing people from poverty. It's not just about meeting people's basic needs.

It is also about freeing people from the worry and stress that goes with poverty or the threat of poverty. It is a matter of financial security; improving people's quality of life, not by giving them more money - they might actually get less in some instances - but by giving them a security of income, so they can know they'll never have to go short of essentials.

Introducing a basic income would be a statement of values and an enactment of those values. It is for societies who don't believe people should be forced to worry about where their next meal is coming from or whether they can keep (or have) a roof over their heads. It is for societies who believe that, provided we have the capability to prevent such want, we should act to do so.

But there's much more! When we have all this advanced technology and massive productive capabilities, should people be spending their lives in jobs they dislike, in jobs that make them feel depressed, in jobs that make them physically ill or mentally stressed? Should any of that be necessary anymore?

Isn't it about time that we treated people with more decency and respect? Is it really too much to ask that, with all the technology of the 21st century, we should be able to organise our economy so that people are able to do jobs they enjoy doing, jobs they want to do rather than jobs they are effectively forced to do?

And perhaps, given a choice, given the opportunity, people could actually be much more productive than they are now.

Capitalism has, in many ways, been rather successful, but it also has very serious drawbacks. Many people hope for an economic future beyond crude capitalism, retaining many of the free market advantages, but discarding the more greedy, selfish, money-grabbing, uncaring aspects of capitalism.

To illustrate the potential future we could develop for ourselves, consider the world of open-source software. For those who are not aware of this, open-source software is software that anyone is free to use, copy, modify and distribute as they see fit.

Very often, to create such software, thousands of

talented and incredibly skilled and knowledgeable people give freely of their time, not for commercial gain, but for the satisfaction of knowing they helped create things that other people find useful or enjoyable.

It was argued - often by people associated with some large and very profitable corporations - that the software written by volunteers would not be of sufficient quality to compete with commercial products. This, however, has turned out to be completely untrue.

In many cases, the complete opposite is the case. If you're using a version of Linux on your desktop computer, for example, instead of Windows, you'll probably know exactly what I mean. I use Ubuntu (a Linux operating system) and it's so reliable, so quick, so well-designed and easy to use, that it seems ludicrous that so many people are still using Windows - which, to me, seems like something that belongs firmly to a previous century.

Open source software can be vastly superior to commercial products, partly because it is made by people who love what they are doing - by people who want to make a contribution - by people who are motivated by doing something good and helping other people. And such motivations can be utilised far more widely than just the world of computer software.

Such benevolent motivations have often been dismissed or ignored in the capitalist era, but they may be recognised, in time, to be far superior to the profit-seeking motivations that currently dominate our economies.

I'm no communist. I'm not saying profit is a bad word. Good companies, making good products, can make a decent profit, with no complaints from me.

The profit motive has often served us well and may continue to do so - but as we advance into the future, it may become relatively less important.

In a future, more advanced, more enlightened society, other motivations may often prove better, more effective - better for individuals and families, better for our economy, better for our entire society, better for mankind and better for the planet we live on.

The desire to make a profit should perhaps at least partly give way to the desire to make a contribution to the world we live in.

Artists, writers, scientists, designers, engineers and many other talented and skilled people can be doing the work they want to do, the work they believe is important - making a contribution, rather than simply earning a living.

A basic income would also help in the rebalancing of our economy, which is currently too far tilted in favour of the well-off - still too much a matter of the haves and have-nots.

To some people, redistribution is a dirty word. It sounds a bit socialist - another word some people don't like. But here's the thing: Even if you don't like the crude idea of the government taking money from the rich and giving it to the poor, then you might still like the idea of the basic income.

The basic income system does not, in itself, necessarily produce much direct redistribution of incomes or wealth - it depends, amongst other things, on the level the basic income is set. But what it does do is help to redistribute market power. It gives people greatly improved opportunities to improve their situations for themselves.

It does this, not so much through the direct

redistribution of incomes, but through the redistribution of negotiating power. With people no longer being forced to work to earn a living, employers will have to entice them to work.

This puts market power where it belongs - in the hands of people, instead of companies or governments. It redistributes dignity. It redistributes political power as well. It gives people more control over their lives. It looks forward to a future of citizens who have more say over how their time is used, rather than merely being workers - units of production - that serve the profit-seeking ends of their employers.

Basic income could herald the development of a more advanced form of economic organisation - building on what is good about capitalism, but turning our economy from our master to our servant.

Finally, I should add something about freedom. The basic income can strike a blow for freedom.

Nominally, we are free people, but people's freedom is limited if they are half-buried under a deluge of economic obligations. People are not fully free, since they can only earn a living within the sometimes onerous restrictions placed upon them by the laws and regulations of the state. They are not free because, to earn a living, they rely on the cooperation of others, especially employers - cooperation that is not always given, even when clearly deserved.

We are greatly dependent upon the state and dependent upon employers - and we each reached that position without our individual consent. The state and some employers, especially large corporations, have too much power over our lives - and the freedom of individuals has been compromised too far.

The basic income would help to restore our freedoms. It would give us each the negotiating power to drive a fairer bargain with potential employers. It would make us less dependent on employers and give us the freedom to say no to them when we feel they fall short of reasonable standards of decency and respect. And the removal of means-testing would greatly reduce the power of the state to snoop into our personal affairs and interfere in our lives.

The basic income would help rebalance our society - limiting the power of the state, providing protection against bullying employers and restoring economic power to individuals and families, where it rightly belongs.

Delivery

Supposing we finally agree that the basic income is a wonderful idea and that it will work, then there are still many issues that need resolving about how it should be introduced.

There are bound to be some people who would urge the seemingly cautious approach of introducing it gradually - perhaps at a low rate to start with and then increasing it as time goes by and as it gradually replaces other benefits - but I think that would be a terrible mistake.

A key feature of the basic income is simplicity - but introducing it alongside all or most of the benefits it is supposed to replace would bring complexity, not simplicity. It would set the whole project off on the wrong foot.

And introducing it at a very low level - a rate which is below the level people would need for mere subsistence purposes - would mean we wouldn't be able to get rid of the old benefits that basic income is supposed to replace. Many of those benefits will have to be retained, because they'll still be needed to stop people going without food or other essentials.

And if those old benefits remain in place, then the bureaucratic machine needed to administer those benefits will still be needed, meaning important cost savings can't be realised. And without those savings, the issue of affordability could become a much more pressing concern.

Many of the main benefits of a basic income are just not going to be realised if it is introduced alongside the benefits it is supposed to replace. Not having means-testing for the basic income, for example, is going to be of only limited value if people still need to be means-tested for other benefits that would bring their income up to a subsistence level.

No, I think there should be a clear D-Day, at the start of a new tax year, on which a switchover will occur. A swathe of old benefits will be abolished and the basic income for everyone introduced on the same day, along with the relevant tax changes.

This might sound drastic, but there's no fundamental reason why it should be a problem. We simply have to sort out, in advance, who qualifies as a citizen of this country and make sure we have their bank account details in the system.

The fundamental simplicity of a basic income system should be used to our advantage. It is precisely because it is so incredibly simple that it can be introduced decisively - and then we can immediately start to reap the benefits, including huge cost-savings, of no longer having to sustain our huge system of means-testing.

It is true that we won't be absolutely sure about balancing our books on day one. We won't know precisely how much extra tax revenue the tax changes will result in - but any balancing that needs to be done, can be done by adjusting the tax regime - just as it is adjusted every year in the budget.

There can and should be careful preparations made for that D-Day event. There can be a long lead up to D-Day. People will need to be informed about the new system - so they know, in advance, how much they'll be getting and what the new tax rates will be. However, the basic income, the abolishment of many old benefits and the new tax regime come as a package. They wouldn't make much sense otherwise.

Part of the reason some supporters suggest the supposedly cautious approach of introducing the basic income at a low level, alongside existing benefits, is that they are somewhat spooked by criticisms of unaffordability.

Most of them not being economists, they aren't always clear in their own minds why the arguments of unaffordability are flawed - or about how they can counter such arguments other than through supporting a cautious approach to introducing the basic income.

Again, they might be concerned about provoking bad headlines - headlines that scare people by talking about plans to 'abolish the state pension' or 'abolish child benefit' or 'abolish disability benefits.' But these are essentially marketing concerns - not good reasons for changing the fundamentals of how a basic income system should operate.

It will need to be explained to people that existing benefits are not being abolished, as such - they are simply being replaced by a new benefits system - one that is better and kinder and less wasteful because it doesn't rely on means-testing.

It will probably help if we call basic income for children, 'child benefit' - then we can say child benefit is being increased, not abandoned. It will probably help to call basic income for pensioners, 'the basic pension' - rather than saying that the state pension is being abolished.

There will be marketing issues and they will need to be addressed - but, in doing so, we mustn't abandon the basic principles that make the basic income such a wonderful idea.

If we try to maintain, for superficial publicity purposes, various existing benefit schemes, along with their expensive and wasteful means-testing regimes, we would be undermining some of the key reasons for introducing a basic income system in the first place.

Simplicity is an essential part of the basic income's fundamental appeal and the source of many of its benefits. Undermine its simplicity and you undermine the whole idea.

No, the basic income should be introduced as a simple system that instantly makes a host of old means-tested benefits obsolete and allows them to be discontinued in bulk.

The introduction of a basic income would be revolutionary. It would bring a new dawn in efficiency, in financial security and improved dignity for all - and it can and should be introduced as a revolutionary change.

This doesn't mean it will bring about great upheaval. There is no need for that. In broad terms, life will go on just as before. People will turn up for work just as before. They'll lead their lives mainly as before - but they'll do so with more choice, more options, more freedom and with less stress and insecurity. There need be no trauma over the switchover. Nevertheless, it is fitting that people should know just how fundamental a change this is.

In my view, this is a fantastic opportunity to make a huge change for the better. I suggest we try to make the most of it!

My Website:

To find out more about my work, including my other books, please visit **www.IMOS.org.uk**

Some of my other books:

Introduction to Economics

Whatever Happened to the Life of Leisure?

Bullshit Time: The Myths and Nonsense of Panel Show Economics

24119597R00043

Printed in Poland
by Amazon Fulfillment
Poland Sp. z o.o., Wrocław